Baby Turkey

FRANCES HOLLOWAY

To order additional copies of this book, contact:
Xlibris
844-714-8691
www.Xlibris.com
Orders@Xlibris.com

ISBN: Softcover   978-1-6641-9546-2
        EBook   978-1-6641-9547-9

Print information available on the last page

Rev. date: 10/19/2021

BABY TURKEY

Frances Holloway

Dedication

This book is dedicated to Baby Turkey. She was the best. For 22 years she was my best friend she was more than a cat she knew when I was happy and she knew when I was sad. So to my best friend. May you rest in kitty heaven

Baby Turkey

A short story about my kitten well, I would say about 21 years ago I was working and, got a call, from a lady saying she heard I was a cat lover and her hairdresser had found this kitten whose mother had been killed by a car.

She was getting ready to call Animal Control. If no one wanted it. I ask for the address and picked the kitten up. She was so tiny. Her little eyes had only been open for a few days. She was so cute.

However, I was a little worried, I didn't know how things would be, taking her home, or I could care for her.

This is Baby
Turkey chilling

This her
as a Baby

As you can see she
likes her picture taken.

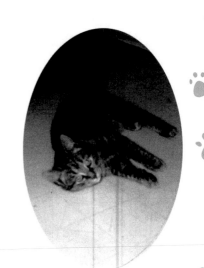

I started to think where am I going to find a bottle to feed the baby with? She was getting hungry and crying so I warmed some milk and spoon fed her with a spoon. It did not take long for her to learn.

I spent time with her, trying to let her know she was not by herself and loved.

For weeks I would take her to work with me. I wasn't sure how my husband would feel about her, but after a while he began to love her just as I did.

Until I knew she could eat and drink on her own. By now she was growing and was all over the place.

My husband would call her Turkey and I called her Baby. So as she grew and had to have shots and her check-up. We were asked, what is your pets name. I said well my husband calls her Turkey and I call her Baby. And that is how she became Baby Turkey. She was so sweet and smart. She knew where she could lay and where she could not.

Baby did not like loud noise nor did she like outside. And if it was wet out she would just tip and get back inside. I told my husband that she minds better than the kids do.

We both enjoyed her for 21 years. She is now in cat heaven with others. Do I miss her? Yes, I do for sure. Will I get another? No, well it's in my plan.

Cats can live up to 35 years, if taken care of. I do not want to get one and it out live me. I know in my heart they would not be taken care of the same way. It would be too hard on the cat to maybe end up at a shelter or worse put to sleep.

At my age I just choose not to do it. I hope it does not sound selfish. I don't mean for it to be. I love animals very much. And I care what happens to them.

As a child I grew up on the river. My Daddy had nets and trotlines all up and down the river. My brother and I would have to run them sometimes. When Daddy had to work far into the night. You see my family worked on a farm. So as many know work is never done.

I the spring there were crops to plant. In the summer and fall there were crops to gather, then in the winter we had to cut wood. Daddy would cut the trees, split the blocks, and we load them on a big truck. If you stacked it right, I think the truck would hold about 5 rick of wood. Sometime we would be gone all day cutting wood. It was very hard work.

When we would drop off the wood to different people, we would get a treat. It was hard growing up in the 40's and 50's.

We learned how to work at a young age. I look back now when we were working in the fields at 7-8 years old. Now kids have phones, all kinds of games they play on them all day. Things sure have changed. Now don't get me wrong, I don't want my little ones to have to work like we did, but I would like to see them get off the couch and go outside and get fresh air sometime.

Well enough about me and my life growing up. Ever though I may one day do a book about my life. May be the last one will be on me. I have to say sometimes I start thinking about some of the things that I have tried and it made me laugh. I have had people tell me to do my life on paper. It would be fun. If and when I do it. There may be a few things I have to leave out "or would I tell all"?

I loved my life after leaving the farm it was very colorful one might say. It was all good, fun interesting. On that note, let me tell you a little about my youngest growing up. The two older ones kept him crying. He always wants to do what they did.

They were not having that. When it came time to hunt Easter eggs they would run in front of him and get the eggs I would take him and kind of show him some of them. Then his sister would watch and run in front of him and take them first. With an empty basket he would go into the house crying. While his sister just laughed. She was a mess 5 years older than the baby.

But she was still my only little girl. Easter has always been nice but let me show you how it started and how it ended.

This is how it started all three happy. But this is the way it ended. My baby crying.

I would talk to her about it. She would say "Well he should have run faster," or he should have seen it. So after it was all over she would hide the eggs and let him find them. Then she would take them all back but she did share later. That was just the way she was.

But as years passed the little brother became bigger than either of them. She would call him her Little Big Brother. They became very close. When my little one was in first grade he would walk to school. I could see the school from my yard.

One day I was out watching for him, and noticed he was not alone. It looked like he was pulling something, that really did not want to go. When he got in the yard he was so happy "Mom, mom look what followed me home. His name is Snowball," he said. It had to be one of the ugliest dogs. It had mange. My little boy said, "Mom can I keep him?" at first I said no! "but he sat down on the ground with the dog looking so sad. I told him we could not keep him because we didn't have a pen. In the end I gave in. We got medicine for him. He stayed in the yard. Every morning he walked to school with my little boy.

Then come home and lay in the yard all day, and when school was out I would see them both coming down the street, it was like the dog knew it was time for school to let out. It was so cute.

My daughter she loved cats. There was a cat that come around our house, she had kittens. My daughter watched the momma cat one day go to the kittens. The next thing I knew my daughter had brought them all into her room. She had made a bed for them in her closet. So here we had a dog outside, and a momma cat with about 7 or 8 baby kittens inside a closet. All three of my children loved animals. The oldest one now he like to fish and hunt.

He was a lot of help around the house too. When I had to work away from home he would cook and make sure the other two had food to eat. All I had to do when I come in was eat and clean up. He would cook but he did not clean up. I was just happy that he did what all that he did. At first when we moved to that town almost every day I would get a call that he was not in school. I would have to leave work, go to school with him. I told him he was going to go to school if I had to enroll and go with him. He was not too pleased with me. He started going and graduated. It was great. I as a mother was very proud of him. I still am proud of him. My first born. To see each, one of my children get through school one less worry for a mother.

Life was good at this point, until my daughter had my first grandson and moved away to another state. That saddened me very much. Thinking I would not get to see him grow up. But she moved back. I was a very happy grandmother.

I just remembered, when my youngest son was 7 years old. About two weeks before Christmas the place where I was working burned to the ground. We had no money. A local church group called Goodfellows heard about what had happened, and brought us food, clothes and toys for my children.

It was very heart warming. One afternoon my baby boy walked in the kitchen, where I was making dinner, with that big smile and big beautiful deep blue eyes. He said I have a present for you. It was wrapped. Then he said it again, momma I got you a surprise. I turned around and looked down at him, and said, "You got me a present?" He said, "Yes as he was holding it I could tell what it was. Just the way it was wrapped, and the way he held it. But I dare not guess what it was it would have broken his little heart. So I said O, baby I don't have any idea what it could be. You could tell he was so excited.

I looked up and there was my daughter. I just knew she was going to say something. But she just laughs and went to her room. I told my little son to put it under the tree so I could open it Christmas.

I think every day he would say, "Momma do you be glad when Christmas comes to open your present?" "O, yes I would tell him." Finely Christmas came. He was up early with it in his hand. To give me my gift. He did not open his until I opened mine. Just made my heart full. He sat there with his blue eyes and smiling. To this day 40 years later is the best gift ever. It wasn't even a new one, but it still had sticker on it. It was brown with flowers on it. Later I ask my oldest son where the dust pan come from. He told me he must have got it a street over from where someone had moved. The landlord had the house cleaned and put stuff out at the curb to be picked up by the trash people. I told my son not to say anything to his little brother. It seems like every day for a while he would say momma did you us your present today. With a smile I would tell him yes baby I did. And I did every day.

My two older children would tell me that the baby was my favorite. I would tell them a mother has no favorite. That each was different and special in their own way.

In the end my daughter and oldest son moved. And it was me and the youngest from then on.

In 2013 my world, was turned upside down. My beautiful only daughter passed away on Easter morning. Things have not been the same. In 2014 one of my granddaughters passed. Then in 2015 my oldest sister passed. So there has been big changes.

Then there is Covid. Peoples love ones are dying all around us. If it wasn't for my faith in God. I would not make it.

People we have to stay prayed up every day. We have to talk to God and be like Jesus ask God to let this pass, and it will. We just have to keep our faith and trust in our Lord and Savior for healing.

For God tells us He will never leave nor forsake us. We have to hold on to that. And trust that He will see us through this. Amen.

Well on a happier note. My birds are back in the yard waiting on me to feed them. Now there are two male cardinals and two females. I was telling my granddaughter about them she said, "I bet one is momma," "my daughter," and the other is my granddaughter that passed.

Then she said one of male's are Jasper, which is her child that passed at birth, and the other male is your favorite brother. I said, "you may be right,"

This Covid mess has stopped a lot of getting together with our love ones. I know like me, you miss being with family.

Two of my great-grandkids spent a lot of time with me and my husband. We would go to the park and feed the ducks and we would have a picnic. Then the boys would play on the swing and slide when I would take them to their house they would always ask when will I come and get them. Now I don't see them much and it is really hard.

They have spent many nights here with us. I will be so glad when this is all over. Well I guess I will say bye for now. Pray some of this give you a smile. I know it has me. It took me back 40 years ago. My baby is 48 now.

My daughter is 51. She passed at 45, and my oldest son is 57.

So it was nice to go back and relive all of this. I tell myself that God must of had a job that only my daughter could do, so I can deal with it. Well enjoy and hope to hear from everyone that reads this. My E-mail is on the back inside cover.

Love all

May God Bless
Be safe
23 Frances Holloway

Special Dedication

Want to say thank you to my husband of 24 years. He has been my rock. This is my 16th book and I have never said anything about him all though in one of my books there is, a picture of him, from the back. So this book goes to my husband and too Baby Turkey Holloway

A Momma's Promise

When a mom says I promise, it is suppose to be forever.

But I remember a promise that I made a long time ago. Then forgot.

But I was soon reminder years later. And it cut through me like a sharp knife.

For I had told my youngest son, that I would never leave him, but I did. He was 11 years old when I made the promise. When he was in his 20's he was still at home, I moved to town. About a month went by and we went to lunch. I thing it was my birthday. With sad eyes, and a broken heart this is what my baby said."

"You told me you would never leave. Then I remembered when he was 11, that I had promised him. It broke my heart, that I his mom had broken my babies heart, and my promise. Even if he was in his 20's, a promise is a promise or it should be.

I sat there in that restaurant watching my grown son, turn into that little boy many years ago. Tears streaming down that sweet face. That soft kind heart of his, now looking across the table from me. With tears from his big blue eyes dripping onto the table cloth.

We both just sat and cried and held one another.

Yes, he was in a grown body, but all at once he was my little baby boy again.

So mom's out there, be careful what you promise your children. You just never know when it might come back on you.

So to my baby son, I am so-so sorry and momma loves you so very much. My baby is 48 now, but I still see my little boy.

Don't want to leave out my oldest son, whom I love so very much. He is 57.

Love to my children
"Momma"

"God is as Close as Your Breath"

Remember as a child growing up. We thought we were lucky for every, good thing that happened then one day we learn, "it was not luck at all, it was God."
> You see God is with us each day of our lives.
> God will use us to tell others about Him.
> We all want to go to heaven but we don't want to die.
>
> Amen.

Frances Holloway

Other Books Published

The Turtle That Lived in the Sand

Little Bit Finds His Kin, Or Does He?

O' Santa, O' Santa, Is That for Me?

A Duck Named "Quack-Quack" and "Huey the Piglet"

Fun Learning

My Little Picture Book #1

My Little Picture Book #2

The Little Elephant and His Friends

One Crazy Chick

All So Tragic

Blackwell's Dysfunctional Family

Letter to My Daughter

Queen Belsie – The Giraffe

Baby Turkey

E-Mail

francesholloway2002@yahoo.com

Printed in the United States
by Baker & Taylor Publisher Services